Creative Doodle Paper

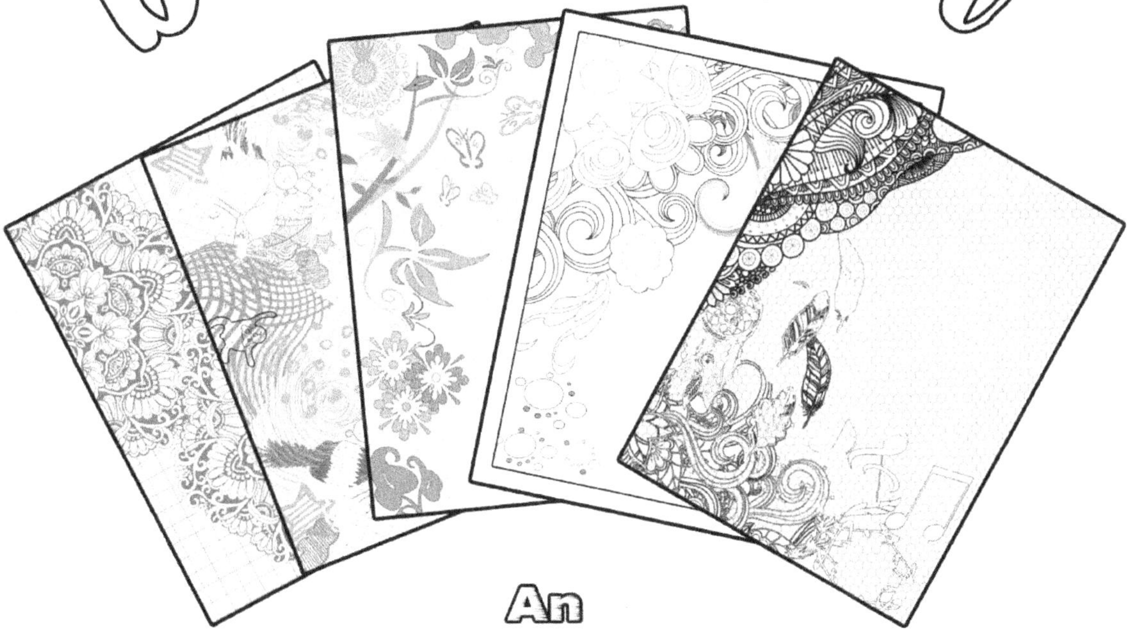

An

EXPLOSION

of Creative Doodle Paper

You Go Girl!!